CHRISTIANS & SOCIOLOGY

DAVID LYON

TO THE CHALLENGE OF SOCIOLOGY...
A CHRISTIAN RESPONSE.

InterVarsity Press
Downers Grove
Illinois 60515

acknowledgements

My thanks are due to several
friends who have criticized and
commented on the manuscript
at various stages, and
also to my wife, Sue,
who did much more than just type
the manuscript when she was
great with child.

InterVarsity Press is the book-publishing
division of Inter-Varsity Christian Fellowship, a
student movement active on campus at
hundreds of universities, colleges and schools
of nursing. For information about local
and regional activities, write IVCF,
233 Langdon St., Madison, WI 53703.

Distributed in Canada through InterVarsity Press,
1875 Leslie St., Unit 10, Don Mills, Ontario
M3B 2M5, Canada.

Quotations from the Bible are from the Revised
Standard Version (copyrighted 1946 and 1952,
Second Edition 1971, by the Division of
Christian Education, National Council
of the Churches of Christ in the United States of
America), unless otherwise stated.

ISBN 0-87784-578-6
Library of Congress Catalog
Card Number: 76-21458

Printed in the United States of America

Contents

64271

Preface: a Christian approach

Sociology is a growing industry. Each year larger numbers of people start courses in sociology, either as a main subject for a degree, or as a component of a course in education, social work, or industry. Of those who are Christians many are quite unprepared for the subtle and persistent tendency of sociology to erode faith and raise doubts. Very few have any idea of how a Christian might approach sociology.

Some, particularly those who are 'insulated' by a fellowship of Christians in church or Christian Union, manage to hold on to their 'faith', but not always in a healthy way. They may just create separate compartments in their lives for faith and study, thus sacrificing their integrity. Others, who would previously have professed to be Christians, but who now find their faith utterly shaken, discard it, feeling that sociological enlightenment and Christian faith are incompatible.

The problem is not always one of a crisis of faith. It may just be that the Christian feels almost schizophrenic because he knows he should see society in relation to God, but for the purposes of his studies he has to look at society in an entirely man-centred way. His faith in Christ and the Bible may be as strong as ever. He may believe in their absolute relevance to sociology, but be afraid to stand up and say so, because he has not worked out in a reasoned way *how* they are relevant. On the other hand, he may turn the seminar paper into a sermon, asserting that God is real, and the Bible's picture of man true, but never understanding the relationship between sociological assumptions and Christian faith. This kind of performance serves simply to confirm the tutor's and fellow-students' opinion that Christianity is a mindless escape from the real world, and will probably be that student's last attempt to 'defend his faith' in the company of sociologists. There is a need to think through both Christian faith in relation to sociology, and vice versa.

This book is intended to help anyone who, for the first time, is facing the challenge of sociology. It aims to show how the subject itself is based on certain assumptions, how Christians can learn from its challenges and deal creatively with them, and how, in time, they might contribute usefully as sociologists.

DAVID LYON

Sociology and Christian faith

The influence of sociology on contemporary thought is undeniable. Sociologists pronounce with seeming authority on all manner of subjects. Educators, lawyers, industrialists and, of course, social workers all turn to sociology in their search for a better understanding of the society in which they live.

The sociological way of thinking ultimately affects the manual labourer, the black neighbour, the street-corner child and his teacher just as much as the professor and his students in the college classroom. But to many Christians it seems a threat, a pernicious dogma which promises to confuse and corrupt.

Often, at first, its true colours are blurred by a veil of polysyllabic sociologese. Once the student is behind the veil, however, and has been initiated into the ritual, it is almost impossible to return to the form of consciousness once thought of as normal. Nothing seems quite the same any more. Not even, for the Christian, his faith.

Yet what is sociology and where has it come from? Even in these days of 'O' level sociology few people know. But still sociologists write and speak with apparent authority on all kinds of subjects. They may affirm, for example, that people do not have a 'self' but rather a succession of roles, or that religion is no more than a response to frustration, anomie or socialization. The effect on the Christian of such pronouncements can be somewhat disturbing. There grows up a tension between his behaviour in academic circles and his behaviour among Christians. His thinking in seminars takes into account only man; in Bible study sessions he may carry on as normal, but find that he is becoming double-minded. He may join fellow-Christians in prayer or discussion, but at the same time, in spite of himself, be somehow standing back from it all, accounting in psychological or sociological terms for all that he and the others do.

There are several ways in which the Christian student of sociology may react. He can switch courses, changing to history (or mathematics or music – it does not matter as long as he has heard that other Christians have successfully completed that course). But this is only to defer facing the problem: the sociological world-view informs so many other fields today that it is difficult to escape for long.

Alternatively, he may continue his course, but with a compartmentalized mind. Work and religion must not be allowed to mix. Sociology becomes a necessary evil (a method of obtaining a qualification), but this 'secular' pastime is not allowed to affect the 'sacred' part of his mind at all, not on a conscious level at any rate. (Our look at the nature of man in chapter four acts partly as a corrective to this view.)

Of these alternatives I think the first is the better. If a Christian honestly feels that he lacks either the equipment or the maturity to deal with sociology, then perhaps he would be better off in another area. But if you feel this way please read on: this booklet may encourage you to carry on your study of sociology, seeing it in the light of your faith and humbly depending on God.

The second alternative does not seem to me at all Christian. To separate the secular from the spiritual is to deny Christ's right to be Lord of one's whole life. It means going back on the declaration of complete surrender that the Christian has made in response to the effectual call of the gospel. Can one who claims the personal rule of his own mind also say 'Jesus Christ is Lord'? The sacred/secular division is always a dangerous one, and can lead to what I call 'super-spiritual worldliness'. This is the condition of a person who can mouth the appropriate evangelical clichés and simultaneously deny them by his life-style, which includes his attitude to study. To accept the authority of sociology during the week and that of the Bible on Sundays is surely to be double-minded. And, as James the apostle warned, the double-minded person is unstable in all his ways.

There is also a sociological reason for the inadequacy of such a view. To split one's roles, so that one has a 'Christian' role, which is different from one's 'sociological' role, is to suggest that there is an incompatibility between the two roles. One cannot think as a Christian when studying sociology, or vice versa. Thus role-splitting implies that Christian values have no place in sociological theory, or that a sociological perspective is irrelevant to Christian faith.

The third and saddest possibility is that the Christian may embrace sociology as a new faith that gives superior understanding. He uncritically swallows all that the lecturers and text-books put before him and dismisses the Bible as no more than an interesting set of human documents.

The last – and, in my opinion, best – option is for the Christian to study sociology with a mind open to the Word of God. The problems raised by sociology *are* often a challenge and sometimes an illumination to the Christian faith, and as such must be faced honestly, not avoided. This is the attitude that I hope the following pages will encourage you to adopt. You will not find all the answers here, but I hope that, at least, the nature of the difficulties will become a little clearer, and that you will realize that you are not the only one to be worried by sociology.

Perhaps the main conflict between today's sociology and Christian thinking is the tendency of socio-logy to 'relativize'. Whereas the Christian believes that there are divine, absolute standards, the socio-logists deny this by pointing to the social and cultural relativity of norms, values and beliefs. Closely related to this is what the American sociologist Peter Berger calls the 'debunking motif'. It turns up persistently in sociological writing and, caricatured, runs like this: 'Common sense and old wives' fables have said ... but sociology finds that ...' Some sociologists do seem to take a perverse delight in unsettling the layman and unmasking his myths, but beneath this surface conflict of values lies a conflict between whole systems of thought.

The Christian and the sociologist have very different starting-points for their thinking and quite different answers to questions like 'What is it possible to know?' and 'Can we know anything?' So when we have sketched the origins of sociological thought, we must return to this question of knowledge, for it is here that any divergence begins and here that the challenges must be faced. We shall then consider the two fundamental areas of debate between the Christian and the sociologist: the image of man, and the nature of his religion.

It must be noted at the outset, too, that sociology is not monolithic. There is great diversity and variety; sociological notions are as numerous as sociologists! Here we shall be concerned with what might generally be accepted as a sociological interpretation of people and things. We shall discuss 'the Christian and sociology' in much the same

13

way as we might discuss 'the Christian and philosophy', recognizing that these disciplines are subject to change and development and that there are movements and individuals who have played a unique part in that development and so deserve separate attention.

Sociology of sociology

If we are to understand the importance of sociology today, we must look at its social, political and intellectual origins. It is not enough to say that sociology is the attempt to 'understand society', because while that is certainly true, it is not an end in itself. The sociologist, however abstract his theory sounds, wants to understand the society in which he finds himself so that he can cope with it, and maybe control or change it.[1] The history of sociology is evidence enough for this.

Sociology is a direct product of nineteenth-century humanism and scepticism, and it must be seen as part of that tradition. Those years threw up

[1] See R. Aron, *The Main Currents in Sociological Thought* (Penguin, 1969). The different desires to change or control society gave rise to different sociologies.

several unique and novel problems, with which man had not previously had to grapple. The impact of industrialization and revolution on Europe had such vast implications for all sectors of society that there was confusion and bewilderment at what had happened. Whole new 'classes' were created as the very basis of society was shaken; old values, customs and allegiances were forsaken, and new ideas, life-styles and institutions took their place. Sociology emerged in response to the need for total social reconstruction in the wake of nineteenth-century upheaval. But the first sociologists themselves were actively involved in that upheaval, and were often radically affected by it.

Revolution

We must glance first of all at the revolution which took place in France at the turn of the nineteenth century. It was the first revolution in history whose supporters based their ideas on the new notion of 'popular sovereignty'. The will of the people, as opposed to the will of God or the king, became the dominant factor. The mass of the people, they argued, must be involved in the political process, in order that their will might be known and done and, hopefully, that 'Liberty, Equality and Fraternity' might be achieved. But how was the popular will to be determined, and how could the masses be brought right into the decision-making process? These problems gave rise to an unprecedented spate of social theorizing.

'Popular sovereignty' brought with it a new sense of identity (a huge group of people living in the same territory under one banner) and a new ideology – nationalism. We must not forget that Italy and Germany, for example, have been nation-states for little over a hundred years. This modern form was something else that had to be understood and explained. The state reaches into the lives of all members of society, and has a great capacity to influence and manipulate the individual, the family and other social groups. The bureaucracy needed to run a nation-state was a novelty, and Max Weber (1864–1920), a German sociologist, explored this area so deeply in his studies that he is still quoted today at the outset of any discussion of bureaucracy. We could safely say, too, that the thinking that began with nation-states was continued in the idea of 'social systems', the grand macroscopic concern of many (especially American) sociologists. But that is to anticipate.

Industrialization

At the same time as the spirit of revolution swept Europe a massive technological revolution, or more accurately, evolution, was taking place, as new methods were employed in production. Once again, the impact was heavy and seemingly irrevocable. The early sociological writers began to realize some of the social implications of industrialization and laid the foundations for the systematic study of its effects on human social life. Contemporary sociologists continue to build on these foundations, studying, for example, the impact of technology in the home. Whole sociological research units are in operation, attempting to assess the effect of television in homes, cars on family life and the automation of various household chores on the housewife.[2]

To talk merely of the direct impact of machines on man is, however, only half the story. A far-reaching effect of industrialization was the creation of a society of urban workers. This has given more impetus than any other event to the development of sociological theory, and is still the root concern of the sociologists of the late twentieth century. The split between 'home' and 'work', for example, was first noticed soon after the emergence of the 'factory system'. This was a division between the 'family' and the 'economy'; or, put another way, the family became a predominantly consuming, rather than a producing, unit. Some have said that from then on, the family was increasingly stripped of its functions. As Christians, we ought to examine and test this kind of statement. This is one of the key areas of debate today. Other related concerns that sociology took under its aegis were 'pre-industrial' society (and now, of course, 'post-industrial' society!), organization theory, industrial relations and a host of others, nearly always linked to the social impact of industrialization and urbanization.

Various important thinkers, such as Owen in Bri-

[2] See, for example, J. D. Halloran, *The Effects of Television* (Panther, 1970).

tain, and De Toqueville, Fourier and Comte in France, tackled these problems with theories which varied in their degree of realism and utopianism. Robert Owen (1771–1858), for example, tried experiments in industrial socialism in his famous 'New Lanark Mills', whereas Fourier (1772–1837) dreamt up 400-family 'phalanxes', which were to be co-operative communities based on the division of labour. In Fourier's scheme (which was never realized) even five-year-old children were to utilize their propensity for getting dirty by being employed as refuse collectors!

But the thinker whose influence has probably been the most pervasive in this area is Karl Marx (1818–83). He saw many features of industrial society which had been overlooked or misunderstood by others. He believed that under the 'capitalist' mode of production men were wage-slaves, because all they could do was sell their labour-power to their employer. They did not control their hours or what they produced. This led to estrangement from the product, from their employers and, with the fragmenting effect of dividing one task into a number of small repetitive jobs, estrangement from their workmates. The nearest English equivalent to the word he used for this estrangement is 'alienation'. Although Marx himself would not have subscribed to a thoroughgoing 'economic determinism', many of his followers have neglected other, more 'humanistic',[3] aspects of his work, and

[3] Humanistic: this is the only time that this word will be used in the sense of 'recognizing man's humanity and dignity'. In

19

have thus injected a low view of man into their social-economic theories. Having said that, the economic 'factor' *is* still the crucially important component of Marx's 'gospel'. It led to his announcement to a rather mystified bunch of trade-unionists and Chartists in 1847 that human history is no less than the history of class struggles, between the alienated worker and his employer or the serf and his lord – the result of conflict between different ways of running an economy.

Industrialization had many more effects. More workers were brought under one roof than in any previous economy. There was specialization and mechanization. Men were brought into new relationships with each other (as fellow workers, as workers to managers, or as managers to owners) and with machines. Different interests were often in conflict, and the resolution of conflict and the amelioration of conditions has frequently catalysed the development of sociological thought.[4]

In Britain, there was a tradition of 'social survey and legislation', linked with such names as Sidney and Beatrice Webb (and the Fabian Society), Charles Booth (1840–1916) and Seebohm Rowntree (1871–1954). They all used material gleaned from statistical surveys of poverty and distress in urban areas to press for legislation on working con-

future, it will be used to describe that philosophy which puts human interests paramount, rejecting the supernatural.
[4] The French sociologist-theologian Jacques Ellul has written about mechanization in *The Technological Society* (Vintage Books, 1973).

ditions, housing, sanitation and so on. The combination of this tradition with a more philosophical one led to the London School of Economics being the pioneer of sociology in Britain.

Sociology developed, then, as a response to the uprooting of social life by revolution and industrialization in the nineteenth century. But why did it take the particular forms that we see today, and how did it eventually achieve such an important status?

Enlightenment to evolution

The intellectual origins of sociology can justly be traced to the eighteenth-century 'Enlightenment'.[5] Supernatural explanations of observable phenomena, including the life of society, were declared invalid and society was studied as a part of nature. This was the new and radical way of thinking which provided the background to the political, economic and social changes of the nineteenth century. The revolution in France led to great optimism that man could completely transform society by his own power and without reference to God, and the rise of 'science' during the century, as the supposed key to all the mysteries of the world and the universe, confirmed this idea in many minds.

Whatever the actual proportion of true Christian believers in the nineteenth century, there was

[5] Humanistic French *philosophes* believed that they had 'enlightenment' as they replaced revelation by reason.

undoubtedly a change in belief within society as a whole. Accompanying the industrialization and urbanization, at which we have already glanced, there was a secularization of the structures of society. Religious practice and institutions (as, for example, the belief that the family is a 'God-given' unit) increasingly lost social significance. At the same time, or maybe a little later, religious thinking also lost social acceptability. A religious (predominantly Judeo-Christian) interpretation was removed, or no longer deemed necessary, when discussing the history and society of man. Although, in retrospect, we might think that some teaching which was described in the last century as 'Christian' was not fully biblical, the point is that a biblically directed world-view was once acceptable as a guide to social life. It was not discounted without consideration, as it usually is now. By the 1870s in England, and before that in continental Europe, a new 'orthodox' interpretation of the world and events, which for want of a better expression could be called the 'scientific' world-view, had gained ascendancy. We shall see, however, that this new way of looking at the world was no less 'religious' than before. It was a matter of changed belief.

As men observed the changes that had overtaken Europe, they saw that science had a large part to play in the formation of the new nation-states, especially in the technological innovations. Those were times of crisis and upheaval, and there was a need for a coherent explanation of what was happening. If science had done so much to produce the world that now existed, then perhaps science could explain that world. As the world was increasingly being tamed by science, so the obsession with being 'scientific' increased. This belief that the methods of science can provide answers to all questions deemed valid by that same science, we shall call 'scientism'.

The clearest example of scientism in sociological theory is the work of the man who coined the word 'sociology', Auguste Comte (1798–1857). He saw history as a unified whole, yet subdivided into stages. He believed that he was living at a time when one stage, the 'theological and military', was dying and another, the 'scientific and industrial', was being born. He called the latter stage 'positive', meaning that science yielded 'positive' results from 'nothing but the facts'. He declared that positive-stage man could not possibly believe in 'revelation', but that he did, nevertheless, need a religion. Comte therefore founded the bizarre and ritualistic Religion of Humanity. Nowadays, this aspect tends to be played down as nineteenth-century eccentricity, but in fact the Religion of Humanity was closely tied to his sociology. He thought that his sociology was rational and empirical, but ignored the metaphysical (or religious) foundation that underlay both his 'scientific religion' and his sociology. It was an institutionalization of the process that the apostle Paul describes in Romans 1 : 25, where men 'worshipped and served the creature rather than the Creator'.

23

It is only in the last few years[6] that large numbers of thinkers have come to accept the fact that behind every 'science' there is a 'meta-science'; behind every scientific hypothesis, a 'paradigm' or framework of taken-for-granted assumptions (otherwise known as 'presuppositions'). Comte presupposed certain 'truths', which he held to be self-evident, such as the falsity of supernatural religion, the inevitability of moral, as well as technological, progress and the efficacy of his method to produce reliable results.

Comte is an important link between the sociology of the 'founding fathers' and that of today. His positive philosophy had a twentieth-century successor in 'logical positivism',[7] which took further his doctrine that men can have knowledge of phenomena only by trying to determine whether or not statements are meaningful. The common thread is that the category of 'revelation' as a source of true knowledge is ruled out from the start.[8] The relevance of all this to us is that logical positivism is closely allied to empiricism, which claims to reject all *a priori* knowledge and rely only on experimentation (with phenomena). These opponents of 'revelation' would assert, therefore, that the Bible

[6] Especially since the publication in 1962 of T. Kuhn, *The Structure of Scientific Revolutions* (University of Chicago Press, 2nd edn 1970).

[7] This philosophy, which attempts to determine whether or not statements are meaningful, rules out religious language as 'non-sense'.

[8] See A. J. Ayer, *Language, Truth and Logic* (Penguin, 1971), for an exposition of this view.

can have nothing to say about the nature of man or society.

Positivism and empiricism have had a big, if not the biggest, influence on the development of twentieth-century sociology. This is most obviously so in the dogma of 'value-freedom' (interpreted as 'ethical neutrality'), which was a leading motif of empiricist sociology (especially American) in the 1940s and '50s. The original notion was Max Weber's *wert-frei*, but it eventually became the sociological justification for ignoring crucial social issues. At precisely the time when there was huge agitation for black equality, there was a conspicuous lack of interest in the sociology of race in the American Sociological Association. Thus, ironically, sociology became insulated from the very society which it was supposed to study.

But we must return to the nineteenth century for a moment. The relation between religion and science was probably the most important single cause of crisis in nineteenth-century minds, and as a 'crisis' it became the theme of many major social thinkers. They all wanted to be thought of as scientists, because it seemed to them that scientific thinking was the only precise, successful and valid mode. Durkheim (1858–1917) for example, who was a professor of philosophy, wanted sociology to establish a non-religious morality now that traditional religion was being discredited. In those optimistic days science seemed to hold all the answers to the problems of life.

It would be foolish to ignore, at this stage, the

impact of evolutionary ideas on nineteenth-century thought.[9] *The Origin of Species* was published in 1859. As it dawned on society that men might somehow be related to apes, one might think that man would have been temporarily dethroned. The Victorians' optimistic faith in man could not be restrained for long, however, and it was soon suggested that man could influence the course of his so-called 'evolution' in a progressive direction. This came to be known as 'social Darwinism' and Herbert Spencer (1820–1903) was its chief exponent.[1]

Comte's system, evolutionary in essence, ended logically enough with the Religion of Humanity, and Herbert Spencer's *Study of Sociology*, which appeared in 1874, completed his work on a system of evolutionary social philosophy which was to replace all previous thought, including, of course, theology.[2] It was all a working out of Pope's old dictum: 'presume not God to scan; the proper study of mankind is man.' To understand the condition of man had become the central concern, and the evolutionary-progressive angle reinforced the belief that man is basically good and has the potential to improve and rule himself without external authority or aid – apart from that of science.

The positivistic-scientific attitude, which still

[9] See J. W. Burrow, *Evolution and Society* (Cambridge, 1965).
[1] See R. Hofstadter, *Social Darwinism in American Thought* (Beacon, 1955).
[2] See D. Lyon, 'Sociology and Secularization', *Faith and Thought*, 102.1, 1975.

colours most sociology today, is one of the main humanistic roots of the subject. It has led to a great emphasis on observation and data, especially among those (often in social psychology) who describe themselves as behaviouristic in outlook. This attitude, which arose, remember, from the belief that science was taking over from religion, probably contributes to the apparent arrogance and authoritarianism of some of today's sociology. Some sociologists still give the impression that they are the high-priests of their religion as they deliver their wisdom with unction and prophetic certainty, incanting the sacred mantras of 'embourgeoisement' or 'ethnomethodology'!

Sociology today

The blind faith in science, so characteristic of earlier thinkers, has been somewhat tempered by the wars and technocratic imperialism of the twentieth century. There is an undercurrent of dissatisfaction in the sociological world with the naivety of making 'final' scientific pronouncements about society, or suggesting that social 'laws' exist for society just as 'laws' such as gravity exist in nature. There is also a growing realization that sociologists, no less than anyone else, make assumptions about man and society and speak from a specific value-position, which naturally colours their perceptions and their thinking. For example, the assertion that man is fundamentally rational (or irrational) or that society is inherently stable (or unstable) is really a world-hypothesis. It is, in other words, a presupposition or belief about the nature of things, which is ultimately determined by one's religious viewpoint. Assertions of this kind are unverifiable, and must be accepted by some sort of intuitive faith. One may say, with Marx, that man's 'natural' state is 'species-being' (that is, unconstrained, purposive activity in work), but this is not observable in the empirical sense. It is an article of faith, a presupposition.

The old notion of 'value-freedom', as used by American sociologists (and some British ones), meaning that they were immune from having presuppositions and that they could be scientifically detached and dispassionate, is a myth. All sociological categories are inherently and inescapably 'value-loaded'. Consider them for a moment. Whether they are *areas* of sociological concern, such as the family, industry or education, or *concepts*, such as 'deviance' or 'socialization', they are bristling with value-positions and value-conflicts. The task of sociology must begin with a recognition of these facts.

Today, there are new 'sociologists of sociology'[3] who would have us theorize self-consciously, not pretending that we are value-free, but deliberately basing our arguments on a foundation of explicit assumptions. The old belief that revelation is irrelevant is probably still as strong as ever, but the emergence of this new, unashamedly committed

[3] *E.g.* A. Gouldner, *For Sociology* (Allen Lane, 1973), or R. Friedrichs, *A Sociology of Sociology* (Free Press, 1970).

sociology may mark the beginning of a fresh opportunity for Christians to show that their assumptions tally with what can be observed in society.

In order to understand how we should react, we must pause at this point and glance back at the social and intellectual origins of sociology, which have already been considered. We said that sociology is an attempt to understand, cope with and control or change society, which grew out of the nineteenth-century crises of revolution, industrialization and changing belief. Macroscopic concerns, such as the great migrations of rural workers to the cities, arose out of the enlarged social group constituting the nation-state. Microscopic concerns, often to do with housing and sanitary conditions, grew out of the 'reform' traditions which began in late Victorian England. Sociology, as it has developed, then, is fundamentally humanistic and scientific. Today's sociologists, however, are gradually realizing two important truths: that the mechanistic models of natural science cannot be transferred indiscriminately to the human or social sciences (they are usually inappropriate); and secondly, that every sociologist inevitably colours his work with certain assumptions or presuppositions.

For various reasons, many Christians in the nineteenth century failed to see the challenge of the intellectual world; this is a trend which we must try to reverse. Firstly, there are many issues which Christians have yet to think about. For example, sociology has much to say about social change, but it is all too obvious that Christians have had very little awareness of how much they are affected by such change and even less have achieved a Christian view of it. Secondly, we need to realize what and where are the conflicts between Christian and sociological thinking. We must understand that much of historical and contemporary sociology is, in its presuppositions, at variance with a Christian worldview, and it is here that we must challenge the prevailing ideas. To take examples again, relativistic sociology produces grand theories about the family and the state, but knows of no reference-point outside either. Sociologists may, for the purpose of analysis, choose arbitrary reference-points within society and may come up with illuminating ideas; but they can claim no ultimate significance for them. Of course, it is true that our knowledge is relative to our situation: we are creatures. But our Creator has revealed truth – including truth about man in society – which is not situationally determined. This we shall look at in the next section.

A word of caution is in order here. Although, as Christians, we must often disagree with sociologists over basic assumptions, this does not mean that all sociological theory is therefore invalid. Far from it! Much excellent work in sociology has been done by non-Christians, and has achieved many God-pleasing results in society. Various social reforms, for example, which have come about as a direct result of the work of sociologists, can only be described as helping man to live as he was originally intended to live. But there is a very long road ahead. If nothing else, the sociology of sociology shows that our understanding of society is at a very elementary stage and that there is a new chance today for Christians to make their contribution from a distinctive biblical position.

Says who?

'The sociologist is the guy who keeps asking, "Says who?"' – Peter L. Berger.

Sociology tends to take one off balance because it probes beneath the surface into things that we take for granted. Many comforting assumptions come under heavy fire from sociologists and this can be very distressing, especially for the unprepared. In this section we shall look at the loosely defined area known as the 'sociology of knowledge', which attempts to locate all knowledge in its social context. This exercise (of 'locating all knowledge') sounds innocuous enough until we notice that the implicit conclusion drawn from such a study is often that the knowledge, because it can be located, is therefore false, or at least only socially relative.

Let's take a well-known example from a generally

discarded verse of 'All things bright and beautiful'. The vision is of the nineteenth-century country squire singing lustily along with his rustic, forelock-pulling labourers in the village church:

'The rich man in his castle,
   The poor man at his gate,
God made them, high or lowly,
   And order'd their estate.'

The bucolic charm of the scene would be rudely shattered by the sociologist of knowledge, who would allege that the squire, the hymn-writer and the vicar were relying for their positions on the hymn, which functioned to maintain the hierarchical *status quo*. The singing labourers were assured that they were divinely appointed never to rise above their station, and would have had any potential revolutionary aspirations dulled. The squire, on the other hand, would simply be confirmed in his security.

One suspects that there could be a good deal of truth in the above example, and it well illustrates the concept of 'ideology', which is very important to the sociology of knowledge. The hymn-writer is the ideologist – acting as the mouthpiece for a particular way of looking at things, and serving a vested interest in society. An ideology is often thought of as something political, but it can be religious, mythological or intellectual as well. The point is that it gives a justification or explanation for some action, reaction, or state of affairs. More often than not, in sociological usage, the notion of ideology implies a distortion. This is particularly true of the Marxian tradition, where bourgeois consciousness has a distorted view of reality, which is based on their socio-economic position.

There are variations in the use of the ideology concept, and one is forced to work out, from the context, what is meant in a specific case. The sociologist would most probably be referring to a defensive screen which a particular group places round itself to justify its activities. For example, in the 1930s, Australia and New Zealand were able to export cheaply vast quantities of butter to Britain. They undercut the British dairy producers' prices, and the farmers had to look elsewhere for an outlet for their sudden surfeit of milk. They hit on the idea of giving free 'school milk' to children – but the 'ideology' they used was their desire to see poor children better nourished.[1]

A more 'political' example, which shows *two* senses of ideology, might be the teaching in the Iron Curtain countries that the abolition of superstitious religion is a necessary precondition of progress. An ideology (in the non-sociological sense of 'a system of ideas') is here being used to try to transfer people's religious propensities to the service of the state. But in a sociological sense, this could be seen as a distorting ideology – rationalizing a political expedient to serve vested interests, in this case, the state. False ideas may be accepted by large numbers of people and, the sociologist would argue, their

[1] I do not vouch for the veracity of this interpretation!

falsity be exposed only by analysis of the social context in which they were found.

Nowadays it is fashionable to include everything that passes for knowledge within society in the study of the sociology of knowledge. In other words, any sort of common sense or inherited wisdom which is used to guide actions in everyday life becomes important to the sociologist, who will try to trace it to its roots and explain it (away?) in terms of its social setting.

It is therefore impossible to escape the scrutiny of the sociologist of knowledge. Nothing is exempt from his examination, and religion is one of his first targets. (This developed directly out of the situation we described in the last chapter, where 'science', during the late nineteenth century, believed that everything could be explained in a scientific way.) The Christian student of sociology can be quite shaken when he discovers that there seems to be a watertight explanation of his religious beliefs, both in terms of the social context of the origins of his religion, and the social forces which led to his own commitment.

The sociologist of knowledge can point to the Roman oppression of the Jewish nation at the time of Christ, and to the fact that the Jews already had a 'Messiah-myth', which made it all the easier for them to latch on to the 'charismatic' figure of Jesus. The unfortunate episode which ended in his crucifixion as a revolutionary who threatened the stability of imperial rule in Jerusalem was soon compensated for by the ingeniously devised

35

'resurrection-myth', which united his hitherto heterogeneous following under a common and emotive banner.

This can be followed up just as easily by explaining 'conversion' in terms of group-conformity in the family or school, or in terms of particular social needs for recognition or status. Once 'converted', continuance within the church is shown to be no more than a response to the ideology of 'fellowship', which is cemented by the common sticker-confession: 'Jesus is alive today!'

However, the majority of people in Britain today have a 'taken-for-granted world', which, though it may contain some Christian ideas, is fundamentally alien to biblical Christianity. This world-view, which has a number of 'self-evident' assumptions, is what sociologists study. But the sociologist of knowledge will always argue that the world-view is socially determined. In other words, the taken-for-granted world of 'reality' is socially constructed, a product of society alone. Yet, ironically, sociologists themselves often have no reference-point outside society. All they can do is make people aware of what they (in the form of 'society') have taught themselves! In actual practice they will always try to do more than this, because, in fact, *they* hold to certain values which, though often implicit, give direction to their studies.

Society says

The sociologist of knowledge asks, 'says who?', thus

challenging any source of 'authority'. He then enlightens the one who dared make a definitive statement, by explaining that in fact 'society says'. Why do we think in the way that we do? The answer, for the sociologist of knowledge, is always to be found in society. Whatever the specific belief, it can be traced back to its social origin and shown to be a product of its time and place, reinforced by social acceptance and the fact that it seems to work.

This questioning spirit tends to breed in the sociologist a certain cynicism and distrustfulness. One is apprehensive about saying anything positive, definite or authoritative in his presence, for fear of being socio-analysed and put into some category typifying unspeakable conservatism. Even as, for example, you express your delight that some friend has managed to land a new job, the sociologist will virtually write off the event as being utterly predictable in terms of social class aspiration, conformity to the group ethos, and the expected response of compromised ideals to the bourgeois carrot.

We have shifted the emphasis here to try to illustrate a point. We began by speaking of the sociology of knowledge as a questioning of socially held belief on the ground that belief also originates in society. Now we are talking about the effect of this 'says who?' spirit in the individual sociologist. I suggest that the distrustful cynicism stems from an implicit rejection of certain values, such as honesty, respect, love and hope. This is not meant as a 'holier-than-thou' attack on sociology in general, but simply a challenge to some who seem to have ruled out the possibility of anyone's honestly holding a set of values which channel and motivate action. Moreover, this is surely *their* view, and not simply what 'society says': so in their own terms it would be invalid.

Sociology says

Although, in my view, sociology chooses to ignore certain features of human social life with which it should be concerned, sociologists still claim a lot for their subject. This is particularly evident in the sociology of knowledge, where, as I have said, the topics include everything that passes for knowledge in society! Most disciplines have made totalitarian claims for their subject at one time or another, and sociology is only the latest to do so. These claims are usually implicit, but when it comes to 'advising' in industry, education, or some other field, they are often quite dogmatic.

Sociology is devastating in its rejection of authority (on the grounds that it is always socially produced and therefore socially relative), but is also extremely 'authoritative' itself! Understandably enough, it is those sociologists who have realized the futility of trying to pursue neutral investigations who are having to expose authoritarian sociology. They have seen that they, with everyone else, hold presuppositions with which they approach sociology in the first place. But it is very difficult to persuade people about this, because sociology has become a form of consciousness in its own right

It has aimed to give a total perspective on social life, thus from the outset excluding other interpretations. We are urged to use our 'sociological imagination' as we paint our 'sociological portraits'. Definite assumptions are made, which transcend that which can be discovered by observation.

Take, for example, the concept of 'functionalism' in sociology. In functional analysis, society is analysed in terms of its internal workings as a system. 'The function of any recurrent activity', wrote Radcliffe-Brown, 'is the part it plays in the social life as a whole, and therefore the contribution it makes to the maintenance of the structural continuity.'[2] Later sociologists, notably Robert Merton, have shown that not *all* functions necessarily *maintain* society.[3] He gave the name 'dysfunction' to those which tended to break down or erode social structures. He also distinguished between 'manifest' and 'latent' functions, the former being conscious and deliberate, and the latter, unconscious and unintended. Thus the manifest function of prohibiting the public sale of pornographic literature would be to suppress immorality, whereas the latent function would be to create an underground black market for the illegal distribution of pornographic material.

The functionalist movement began as a reaction to a crude evolutionism which tried to explain social

[2] A. R. Radcliffe-Brown, *Structure and Function in Primitive Society* (Cohen, 1952), p. 180.
[3] R. K. Merton, *Social Theory and Social Structure* (Free Press, 1957).

39

institutions in terms of their 'primitive' origin. But functionalists chose to ignore the question of origins altogether, and view society as a system in which beliefs and practices play a functional part. This, in turn, suggests that a 'normal' society is a non-haphazard structure which 'lives' like an organism.

Later functionalists ignored other aspects of social life as well as origins. The obsession with function may lead to a complete disregard of intention. For example, restricting the study of a given custom to its social function may lead to distortion, if the intention with which that custom was begun has been ignored. While the analysis of function may throw light on some opaque feature of social life, it may, by concentrating on that, obscure intention, or, possibly, responsibility and accountability. It can also lead to a devaluation of, say, Christian teaching on the family. We may say that marriage has (among others) a sexual function. The sociologist may point out, however, that many unmarried people also indulge in sexual activity. But he will go on to say that, because the majority of pre-marital intercourse takes place between partners who intend to get married anyway,[4] and because the majority of divorced couples remarry,[5] marriage as an institution is as popular as ever. It is hardly worth pointing out that Jesus Christ was

[4] M. Schofield, *The Sexual Behaviour of Young People* (Penguin, 1965).
[5] R. Fletcher, *Family and Marriage in Britain* (Penguin, 1969), p. 143.

not referring to common-law marriage, or serial monogamy, when he appealed to the *creation* order for marriage in Matthew chapter 19!

We could quite legitimately argue that sociology itself can be an ideology, an example of false-consciousness. The very relativism of sociology means that there is a distortion of the truth about man and society. On the assumption that everything, including knowledge, is socially relative, the sociologist makes surprisingly bold assertions. For example, he might say that a concept or a behaviour pattern becomes 'human' only through repetition and familiarity. But is this only a demonstration of his blindness to absolutes and to givens? The Christian sociologist would want to 'assume' that there is true knowledge – and on that basis affirm that there are permanent and inherently human concepts such as purpose and responsibility. But, then, what right have Christians to counter the claims of the sociologists? How dare Christians assert anything?

God says

We must make our Christian position clear from the outset. There is an increasing concern at the moment with the ideological aspect of social science, and some sociologists do make their assumptions explicit. This is helpful, of course, because then at least we know what we are arguing with.

Lucien Coletti, for example, contending for Marxism as *the* social science, states, 'It is the

41

analysis of reality from the viewpoint of the working class.'[6] In the same way, we must make our distinctive viewpoint explicit.

What do we believe to be true, and *why* do we believe that certain things are true? It is clearly not that Christian ideas are socially acceptable – because the majority do not believe them! Jesus' teaching contains a lot of hard sayings which go against the drift of modern culture. It is really impossible to account fully in sociological terms for a change in belief, especially in a case such as that of Paul the apostle. Everything that he had been taught in his strict Jewish sect militated against his becoming a follower of the 'Way', and he actively pursued a course of attempting to annihilate the early Christians. He was highly intelligent, perfectly rational, and to all appearances normal, both before *and after* the encounter on the road to Damascus. The group he was with at the time were 'anti-Way', and yet from that day on he was completely changed. His world-view, and hence his life-style, were completely different, although what he now believed could hardly be described as socially acceptable!

Perhaps, while on the subject of conversion, we ought to mention William Sargant's famous 'psychological' debunking of conversion in *Battle for the Mind*. He argued that conversion was nothing but bringing people into a hyper-suggestible state, and brain-washing them into Christian belief.

[6] R. Blackburn (ed.), *Ideology in Social Science* (Fontana, 1972).

His aim was to show that what some thought was a divine, spiritual experience was only a product of human manipulation, and therefore to talk of the spiritual was to be deluded. As Martyn Baker has pointed out, however, 'this aim is similar in nature to trying to show that the paints Picasso used were of such and such a hue, and of such and such an intensity – and therefore his works of art are contrived and valueless'.[7]

The naturalistic sociologist uses exactly the same type of argument as Sargant, and will also ignore (as Dr Lloyd-Jones points out in his critique of Sargant[8]) the historic and supernatural aspects of Christianity. Peter Berger uses similar language to Sargant's when he writes that 'the possibility [of conversion] increases with the degree of instability or discontinuity of the plausibility structure [that the person is currently holding]'.[9] He is not, in this instance, attacking religion, but it is clear how, when their words are taken out of context or stripped of qualifying clauses, one could understand social scientists to be saying that conversion is nothing but a sociological or psychological phenomenon.

Christian belief, however, is quite distinctive. This is true of Christian belief about 'conversion', and, more directly related to this section, about

[7] Martyn Baker, 'The Psychology of Conversion', *Faith and Thought*, 101.2, 1974.

[8] D. M. Lloyd-Jones, *Conversions: Psychological and Spiritual* (IVP, 1959), pp. 21 f.

[9] P. L. Berger, *The Social Reality of Religion* (Penguin, 1973), p. 58.

God's being the final authority and reference-point for our view of the world. Christians believe that God has shown himself to man in several ways. This 'self-disclosure' is both general, in the personality of man and in the world outside, and special, in Jesus Christ and the Bible. The general revelation of God in the world points to God's 'eternal power and deity' (Rom. 1 : 20) and his invisibility. In its rationality and reality the world (or universe) reflects these attributes. Because the world created by God is rational, the study of it has meaning. Moreover, the fact that he made it means that individual lives, as significant parts of the whole creation, have purpose. This much is known to everyone, although they may deny or distort it. (In the next section we shall look at God's self-disclosure in the personality of man.)

The argument so far may appear to be circular, and as such, closed and self-validating. God's revelation, however, claims to be the truth of what is. Jesus, referring to the Word of God, claimed that it was truth: 'Thy word is truth.' Not only that, he also claimed to *be* the Truth. These things are open to questioning and scrutiny. Jesus was fully human: he sweated, wept, and was hungry, angry, compassionate and loving. His life was consistent with his claims, his death in line with his predictions, and his resurrection as fully attested as a historical fact as any other in the contemporary period. Jesus perfectly and consistently showed the character of God to those around him, because he was fully God. It is not to anyone that we could say, as Peter did to Jesus, 'You are the Christ, the Son of the living God.'

Similarly, we may examine the Bible's validity. We must ask, does the Bible give a consistent picture which correlates with historical reality? Does it give satisfactory answers to questions about the nature of man and about the everyday problems of life in society? Our answer is 'yes'! The Bible is verbal and contains communicable truth about God and his relationship to creation, so we may expect answers. Only the Holy Spirit makes understanding possible in such a way that lives are changed by the truth, but there *are* things in the Bible which underline the truth of *what we already know* from the created world around – so in that sense it is testable by an 'uncommitted' person.

The 'committed' person, on the other hand, derives his Christian certainty from the object of his belief, God himself. He believes that God has spoken in an authoritative and absolute way, and he can see that biblical statements tally with what he sees around him. Human nature, for example, is not socially relative, but universally and fundamentally in opposition to God – and this religious attitude determines all others. He sees wars all over the world, for example, as symptoms of this underlying enmity to God (James 4 : 1–4) – conflict in society arising from the nature of man.

Moreover, the Bible itself contains the principles by which it should be interpreted. We can study it in an integrated way, because it is internally consistent, and we can compare scripture with scripture to obtain a whole perspective. Major themes occur throughout the Bible, and if these are borne in mind, much light is thrown on the book as a whole, so that God's plan for mankind in history and society can be seen in clear relief. Two such major themes are the faithfulness of God and, in contrast, the sinful fickleness of man.

We shall return to the 'sociology of knowledge' context for a moment to consider the Old Testament narrative, and see how inadequate the crude 'sociology of knowledge' approach is in explaining the history of the Jews. The backdrop to the unfolding drama was always a pagan culture. God spoke to his people repeatedly, through his prophets, telling them who he was, what he expected of them in terms of faith and obedient behaviour, and what they, in turn, could expect of him. The two 'major themes' exampled above appear again and again: God was faithful, and man was fickle; but even through centuries of exile in the middle of completely alien cultures the 'chosen people' survived, *and a large group always emerged still believing in the same God!*

The commands of God were always socially unpopular – so why did the people go on believing them? The pressures to conform to the beliefs and practices of the surrounding cultures were very strong, yet only a certain number capitulated to them – why? The Christian must reply that the commands given were not socially determined: but rather spoken into the situation by an absolutely free God who had repeatedly proved his trust-worthiness as well as his holiness. Although the social pressures to conform to prevailing cultural standards are extremely strong, as we would be the first to admit, there is a stronger external power which enables resistance, both in the day of the Old Testament prophets and in the late twentieth century.

We have travelled a long way rather quickly in this section, but I hope that the question of 'says who?' has at least been partially answered. As Christians, we believe that there is knowledge which is undetermined by any social context, since it has been given, as it were, from outside. This is not to say, of course, that there is no human factor in the Bible. Men with distinctive styles and per-sonalities wrote from within specific social contexts. But the words they wrote were always God's words, and as such, authoritative and infallible. (On this point, I cannot do better than refer the reader to the best short introduction to the subject of the Bible: *The Book that Speaks for Itself* by R. M. Horn.[1]) The fallacy is to say, 'Men wrote the Bible, therefore it is fallible.' For, as God said to Jeremiah, 'Behold, I have put my words in your mouth.'[2] Another mistake is to say that, because God's Word was spoken into a certain historical, social milieu, it is irrelevant today. J. A. Motyer smashes this mis-conception in his commentary on the prophecy of

[1] R. M. Horn, *The Book that Speaks for Itself* (IVP, 1969).
[2] Jeremiah 1 : 9.

Amos – who, by the way, could be seen as the first biblical sociologist![3]

The self-disclosure of God yields principles and criteria for evaluating all ideas which originate in a purely human, social source. Any analysis of reality which has a different starting-point may contain certain features which are true and important for the well-being of society (because God *has* disclosed certain things in a general way to all men), but it must always be judged in the light of God's Word.

If what I say is true, then as Christians we have a duty to study God's Word in the way he has directed, and to apply the principles to specific theories and situations. Our sociological thinking must be shot through with the assumption that neither the individual nor society is the final arbiter of knowledge. God must have not only the last say – he must have the first.

[3] J. A. Motyer, *The Day of the Lion* (IVP, 1974).

Homo sociologicus

Man is always the central concern of the sociologist: man as animal, man in groups, man in society. So the question of man's nature, or rather man's 'image', is of crucial importance to sociological theory. This has been realized since the beginning of sociology, and was, one could argue, the reason why the need for sociology was seen in the first place.

Other disciplines, such as political economy (now known as economics) or biology, seemed to give only a partial view of man, which imbalance sociology was designed to redress. What was not appreciated (and this is often still true today) was that sociology cannot give a 'total' view of man either. It is, after all, only the study of man *in interaction with his fellows*. Sociology frequently gives the impression that other aspects of man are some how less important, or that they can be interpreted from a sociological angle.

This does *not* mean that the sociological study of man is *ipso facto* invalid, but rather that it should be seen as a limited perspective on man, not a total one. It is, I believe, a very important aspect, which biblical Christians have ignored for too long, to the detriment of the church. We shall take a brief look at some forms of *homo sociologicus* which appear in social theory, and try to contrast these with the biblical view of man, especially as he is in his relationship to society. Before proceeding, however, I must point out that this is *not* an attempt at an exhaustive critique of sociological views of man, but rather a tentative and impressionistic survey of common themes in sociological writing.

Man as malleable

The most common feeling that one has about the sociological image of man is that man's nature is essentially plastic. The raw material of physiological apparatus is moulded into social shape by a kind of disembodied entity known as 'society'. Many writers have outspokenly criticized this social determinism, but the idea still lies behind many sociological statements. Only a few years ago, Professor Cotgrove (whose introductory book is standard reading in many places) wrote: 'It is perhaps a somewhat exaggerated analogy to liken individuals to puppets, pulled by social strings, and acting out their parts written for them by society. But they have come to know their parts so well that they are no longer aware of the pulls and pushes, and unlike puppets an internal machinery has taken over and moves them from inside.'

'Socialization' is a big word in sociological thought, and it sums up this view. In most definitions, socialization is 'the transmission of culture' and often sounds as mechanical a process as the phrase implies. Sociologists might argue that man is only minimally determined by his biological make-up, and therefore maximally influenced by his surrounding culture. Man knows nothing, it seems, that he has not learnt in society. Sociologists are often keen to minimize the idea of 'instinct', opting instead for 'learnt behaviour', but as we shall point out, this dichotomy is a false one, having developed out of eighteenth-century empiricist ideas of knowledge.

Many of the words used by sociologists imply that each individual starts out in life as something empty or neutral, which is filled up with a stock of culture, and directed in a particular way. This is a modern version of Locke's old notion of the '*tabula rasa*' – the 'clean slate' mind which has not yet received any outside impressions and experiences.

Another word is 'internalization', which suggests that everything that makes up the individual personality comes from outside, from society. Man is made in the image of society. In this view he is man because he shares with others a common culture, which is a relative, on-going historical entity.

Sociology gives Women's Lib its impetus. While we share some of their concerns, they do overstate their case. For example: 'One is not born, but rather becomes a woman. No biological, physiological, or economic fate determined the figure that the human female presents in society; it is civilization as a whole that produces this creature, intermediate between male and eunuch, which is described as feminine.'[1] Perhaps the only comment that needs to be passed on this is the reminder that they have not yet come to terms with their different shape, their beardlessness, and their capacity for child-bearing.

But we need to isolate a little more the different sociological perspectives which give rise to this claustrophobic determinism, this feeling of being trapped in a web of social networks. Gibson Winter[2] has distinguished between three such categories, and we shall look at his general (and much simplified) scheme.

Firstly there is 'behaviourism'. Its adherents believe that responses are conditioned: either instinct stimulates to produce a response which has calculable effects, or external (*e.g.* social) forces produce internal effects. Behaviourism, as an explicit doctrine, is more common to psychology, but represents the cruder thinking of some positivistic sociologists. If their thinking were right, social 'control' could be obtained by the manipulation of

[1] Simone de Beauvoir, *The Second Sex* (Penguin, 1972).
[2] Gibson Winter, *Elements for a Social Ethic* (Collier-Macmillan, 1966).

sanctions. Arthur Koestler has described this kind of thinking as 'ratomorphic'[3] – meaning that, in theorists' minds, man is thus reduced in status to the image of a rat in a laboratory maze.

'Functionalism' is the second category, and we have already defined it in the previous section. Once again, if this is *the* perspective of the sociologist, his theories will be less than human. If society is nothing but a system, to be regulated and controlled by 'functional adaptation', then what has happened to the real needs and even the thoughts of men? If social conflict is seen as 'structural strain', then what can one say about basic incompatibilities of interests and values?

The third perspective is that of 'voluntarism', which has to do with the motives of men and groups in society. Sociologists of this school are occupied not necessarily with self-confessed motives, but with attributing certain drives and motivations to groups who may not be aware of them. This is often political in thrust, and characterizes the work of Marx and Weber in particular. The stress here is on the variability of interest and outlook according to milieu, and sometimes on the role of struggle in social change. Values and interests become socially relative, depending upon the society or part of society in which they are found. Thus Weber, for example, suggested that the spirit of capitalism was strongest in societies imbued with 'the Protestant Ethic'.

What are the implications of these views? If

[3] A. Koestler, *The Ghost in the Machine* (Pan, 1967), p. 30.

society is responsible for the creation of man, then it is responsible for *everything*, not just what is socially acceptable. Society must also be responsible, therefore, for crime and deviance. So we find that the notion of individual responsibility has been widely abandoned in favour of social responsibility. Some contemporary radical 'new criminologists' go beyond this idea, and plead for a society that does not have the power to 'criminalize'. This is a logical conclusion from the assumption that man's nature is 'neutral', and that he becomes man only as society moulds him. All values become historically and socially relative, therefore, and even Christian freedom becomes an inappropriate idea.

But the incidence of criminality is disturbing, viewed sociologically. Different studies have shown that, for example, crime increases with each decrease in educational level.[4] Some social groups are positively inducted into criminal norms, and it is not easy to apply straightforward praise and blame with respect to their obedient conformity. Moreover, as there are so few magistrates (if any) from within, say, 'working-class' culture, it is not surprising that misunderstanding is rife.

Social, or structural, sin is a phenomenon that has been sadly neglected by most Christians in recent years, and sociology does expose the crying need for a radical biblical understanding here. Hopeful signs that there may be new Christian insights in this area include Behm and Salley's book *Your God is Too*

[4] *E.g.* L. MacDonald, *Social Class and Delinquency* (Faber, 1969).

White.[5] They show that the role of Christianity was firmly established in relation to the oppressive institutionalized forces which denied basic human rights to blacks in the United States. Blacks have been made to feel that Christianity is synonymous with white exploitation, dehumanization of blacks and the perpetuation of white domination. In this case, gross social sin was supported, and in some instances even justified, by Christians. We shall return to this point below.

There is clearly, then, a *structural* incidence of various forms of crime, delinquency and injustice, which is measurable, and which must be understood if the notion of 'justice' is to be retained in the legal system. Some sociologists, however, have worked, not with an objective, but a subjective notion of deviance. They are known as interactionalists, and contribute to the 'new criminology' mentioned above. Their concern is with the mutual labelling of people in society as they *interact* with each other. For example, as a teenage delinquent begins to be labelled as such, he responds by conforming more and more to that label. 'Deviance' is no longer an act, but a process, and the question of the individual's responsibility or accountability is discarded as a non-question. What needs to be changed, in the interactionists' view, is the 'system', that, by labelling, 'produces' criminality.[6]

So is man's nature simply plastic? Is he nothing

[5] Lion Publishing, 1973.
[6] I. Taylor, P. Walton and J. Young, *The New Criminology: For a Social Theory of Deviance* (Routledge, 1973).

but the sum of his roles? Is the individual just the palimpsest of the social networks in which he lives? Is crime and deviance only a social construct, and man's nature somehow neutral? These are very often the implications of a 'man as malleable' sociological perspective and, as such, are plainly inimical to Christian presuppositions.

Man as master

According to another view, *homo sociologicus* is powerful rather than plastic. He is active and self-determining, with a self-conscious idea of his aims. In Winter's scheme, this is a fourth category – of 'intentionality'. Man is seen not in terms of cause, function or interest, but intention. He is conceived of as transcending the forces which impinge on him: stepping outside his succession of roles. In this view, Berger writes, far from being puppets, 'we have the possibility in our movements of looking up and perceiving the machinery by which we have been moved. In this act lies the first step towards freedom.'[7]

There is a variation on this theme, however, that can be as worrying as the rigid social determinism of the older positivistic school. In this view man can free himself only in a collective community, by joining hands with others to change the *status quo.* Amitai Etzioni, who is one proponent of this kind of view, suggests that the social sciences, which provide much of the 'self-consciousness', should also

[7] P. L. Berger, *Invitation to Sociology* (Penguin, 1970).

give guidance about the direction of social change. Others write about a 'sociological ethic' which would give a pattern for research and action.[8]

Once again, it is clear that a *sociological* ethic is not enough. There is always an *intellectual* or a *religious* presupposition behind each sociological ethic. While it is good that a sociologist be aware of the moral implications of his work, one would still want to know *where* he finds his 'morality'. If the authority, again, comes *only* from within society, we are trapped – condemned to a 'freedom' prescribed by sociology, which could manifest itself as anything from totalitarianism to anarchy. A sociological ethic, ultimately, is simply one more manifestation of man's attempted autonomy which has its roots in Eden, where the act of fruit-eating symbolized man's decision to be his own arbiter.

Intentionality, then, or 'Man as master', does allow the possibility of positive action resulting from value-convictions, and it does allow for authentic individual existence, as opposed to social conformism. Of course, we must not forget that there *are* social constraints on thought and action, that roles and social location are a component of human make-up, but the intentionalist viewpoint allows us to see that man is more than his roles.

Marxian sociology, in some of its popular forms, tends to unite the two notions of 'malleable' and 'masterful' man in an uneasy combination. According to this persuasion, man is 'determined yet

[8] *E.g.* L. Sklair, *The Sociology of Progress* (Routledge, 1974), or R. Friedrichs, *A Sociology of Sociology* (Free Press, 1970).

determining'. 'Man as world-produced derives his conceptual apparatus from his social matrix; man as world-producing is able to recast, reject, reflect upon his world and his consciousness, and as he effects changes in that world, so does he alter the external reality from which he derives further categories of thought.'[9] This is an existentalist or phenomenological Marxism – but it is still a closed system, part of a 'total' philosophy, which has 'society' always at the boundary-line of perception.

Man as image of Maker

The abiding sociological dilemma (which is really a philosophical question) arises from the frustration of the desire to obtain a *total* perspective on man, because of man's inability to 'step outside' and see himself in this 'whole' way. However hard he tries to avoid it, the sociologist is always a participant observer. He is always 'involved' in the society he is observing. Contemporary sociologists put great faith in their methodology, some of which is very sophisticated, and often does yield new insights, but the most ingenious methodology will still not provide the ability to 'step outside'. The hope that sociology will provide a *total* perspective can never be realized.

We shall now reconsider some of the problems we have been discussing, but this time in the con-

[9] P. Walton, *From Alienation to Surplus Value* (Sheed and Ward, 1972).

text of a biblically directed view of man. Ecclesiastes, curiously enough, is a great source of reassurance when one is faced with the problem of wanting to see man as a whole being, but all that is apparent is inconsistency, inequality and lack of freedom. The writer's approach to observable situations such as the existence of 'righteous men to whom it happens according to the deeds of the wicked' was to apply his mind to wisdom. And wisdom, he knew, is in the Word of God. 'Then I saw', he said, 'all the work of God, that man cannot' (*i.e.* by un-aided reason) 'find out the work that is done under the sun.'[1]

As Christians, we must maintain that the total man cannot be seen except in the light of God's revelation. Now, this kind of phrase has caused difficulties throughout the history of the church, so we must try to explain a little more what it means. The Bible always speaks of man *in relation to God*, never as isolated. There is a repeated emphasis on man's religious orientation as being the clue to his humanity. The first statement about man that Scripture contains is, 'Then God said, "Let us make man in our image, after our likeness."'[2] This does not tell us about his physiological, psychological, sociological, or any other '-ological' aspect of his make-up, but simply establishes the 'whole man' as the 'image of the Creator'.

This, however, begs further questions, the first of which is, 'What about the Fall?' It is all very well

[1] Ecclesiastes 8 : 14, 17.
[2] Genesis 1 : 26.

to speak of man *created* as God's image, but doesn't the Bible speak of an alienation from God, stemming from man's rebellion in Eden? This is true, and moreover, there are many indications of the completeness of the Fall in both Old and New Testaments (such as Psalm 14, or Romans 3 : 23). Man is described as 'lost', 'dead' and 'at enmity with God'. And yet in spite of this total corruption, man is still described as 'man', in Romans 2 : 3, for example. So there is still some element of 'humanity' in man, even after he has lost his oneness with God, and his original righteousness at the Fall.

Another problem concerns the Christian, whose 'new self' 'is being renewed in knowledge in the image of its Creator'.[3] The grace of God restores the image in the Christian, and so it does seem that there remains something on which restoration work can be done, even in spite of the absolute nature of man's sinful separation from God. And we must admit, too, that some people manage to live moral, law-abiding lives, and have harmonious relationships with others without ever having been made aware of the grace of God. It seems that the concept of the 'image' is a very slippery one.

We dare not minimize the effects of the Fall, or sin, by saying that man is somehow partly good and partly bad. Man's separation from God is total, and sin has twisted and warped every area of his life. We must equally avoid implying that the 'good deeds' of Christ-rejecting people bring them any nearer to God. That would be to minimize the im-

[3] Colossians 3 : 10 (New International Version).

pact of the grace of God in the life of the sinner. But this is merely to underline the fact that there are problems. Problems of freedom and determinism, and problems of morality and law, all raised by the question of man's nature or 'image'.

Theology has sought various ways out of these apparent contradictions, no one of which has been altogether satisfactory. A popular idea is that of 'common grace', by which it is said that God holds man's total corruption in check, restraining evil that would otherwise be destructively released. Abraham Kuyper,[4] for example, sees common grace as part of the 'image' by which God limits the extent of evil in the world.

This doctrine would also account for the great achievements of man in society, the scientific discoveries, inventions, artistic creation, and so on. Others have suggested that the conscience is the means of limiting corruption, but in opposition to this, the Bible plainly states that the conscience itself has been twisted by the Fall.[5] It can be weakened or hardened according to the inclination of the individual or the moulding of society.

We shall not spend time here discussing the other attempts to account for the good in the world, linked to the idea of the 'image'. We can point out, though, that contemporary cultural thinking, such as Greek philosophy or humanistic individualism, has sometimes influenced the direction of Christian thought. A notion that has thus been overlooked (or

[4] Abraham Kuyper, *Lectures on Calvinism* (Eerdmans, 1931).
[5] *E.g.* Titus 1 : 15.

avoided because of its propensity to misinterpreta-tion) is our 'common humanity'. The Dutch theo-logian Berkouwer, who draws attention to this writes: 'In considering the fallen estate of man there is indeed more reason for us to reflect on this social component than on the preservation of his understanding and will.'[6]

He suggests that to limit the 'image' to a list of 'attributes' as some have tried to do is both arbitrary and individualistic. In his view (which is most attractive) man's humanness is preserved in his in-numerable man-to-man relationships. Even when man is alienated from God, he is not alone in the world. In society there can be beautiful, meaningful relationships which cannot be explained by the idea that the 'image' is simply a remnant of the original understanding and will in individual men. As he writes, 'When God in his grace preserves man's humanness from demonization, from complete dis-integration in mutual enmity, He does this in the relationships of society. It is, and remains, one of the most striking features of the actuality of fallen man that we see relationships between man and fellow-man function in the midst of the corrupting power of sin, which certainly is directed especially against society and any feeling of responsibility to wards the other.'[7] It is in spite of this common humanity, of course, that man sins. This is due to the sin which is the attitude of rebellion towards God which has characterized man since the Fall

[6] G. C. Berkouwer, *Man: the Image of God* (IVP, 1973).
[7] *ibid.*

62

This alienation in the depths of his being is the root of all other alienations in society.

Total man

The biblical view is that total man is the 'image' of God. This wholeness allows for no splitting of man into body and soul or any other divisions. In fact, it may be more helpful to think of the heart as the core of man's being, epitomizing his unity and wholeness. The proverb exhorts 'Keep thy heart with all diligence; for out of it are the issues of life'. Our Lord, too, said, 'What comes out of a man is what makes him "unclean". For from within, out of men's hearts, come evil thoughts . . .'[8] There are no 'higher' or 'lower' parts of man; he is one.

The total, whole man is religious. Religion is not an aspect of his life, rather it *is* his life. His humanness depends upon his religion. The horizontal aspect of life cannot be fully appreciated until it is seen in the light of the vertical relationship with the Maker. Psalm 139 expresses the amazement of the man who discovers that no earthly relationship can be seen in isolation or abstraction, that he is not autonomous or answerable to himself. Right from his mother's womb there is the vertical as well as the horizontal relationship: 'Thou knowest me right well.' Thus God's revelation directs us to total man in his relation to God.

[8] Proverbs 4 : 23 (AV); Mark 7 : 21, 22 (New International Version).

A word about freedom is necessary at this point. Again, we shall not spend time discussing the philosophies of freedom, but must rather try to outline the threads of the arguments. Much hot air has been emitted in various controversies about the alleged free will of man, but very often the biblical perspective has been eclipsed by non-Christian thinking. The non-Christian tends to polarize 'freedom' and 'compulsion' or 'determinism'. Valuing the notion of freedom, he seeks 'freedom of speech' or of conscience. In other words, he seeks an end to compulsion. Biblical thought, however, posits 'freedom' as the state the Christian finds himself in when the Truth has set him free.[9]

The Bible freely acknowledges that man performs self-willed, spontaneous acts, but asserts that nevertheless he is enslaved to sin. He is not, therefore, a *tabula rasa* before continually new possibilities of right or wrong. Man is responsible for his actions and words, but his capacity for making decisions cannot be called freedom, because he is under the dominion of sin. Christian freedom is not something formal like 'academic freedom', that is, simply a 'being free' *from* something. In general, freedom from a particular rule or pressure is merely *outward*, and therefore peripheral; Christian freedom, however, is a dynamic *inner* quality: the very essence of the life of a person who is 'in Christ', free to do right and to please God.[1]

[9] John 8 : 32.
[1] The Puritan, Samuel Bolton, has some good expositions of

The sociology of sin

Returning now from our necessary theological digression, we find that several important insights have emerged, which can inform our Christian sociological perspective. Tracing the biblical presuppositions about man gives us a foundation from which we can not only be critical of many sociological assumptions, but also begin positively to assert the value of our Christian view. And as Christians we will find that our sociology, all too often, is an examination of the effects of sin on society.

Many sociologists would, of course, be very critical of such an idea. The suggestion that sin, or evil, exists in man is repugnant to them. Professor Abrams, for example, in his book, *The Origins of British Sociology*, criticizes a nineteenth-century sociological questionnaire, which contains the implicit assumption that strikes are caused by the economic self-interest of workmen. He says that this idea is at odds with a good deal of recent industrial sociology: but he himself thus implies that therefore modern industrial sociology can dispense with any consideration of economic self-interest. This betrays an underlying *religious* view, that evil is not innate, but rather is caused by social-environmental factors.

Sin in society may be minimized in other ways, too. The famous Kinsey report on the sexual behaviour of the American male is a good example.

the Christian freedom theme in *The True Bounds of Christian Freedom* (Banner of Truth, 1965).

Certain patterns of behaviour were observed, and classified as social norms. Combined with the naturalistic assumption that there are no universal or absolute norms which ought to be followed, this led to further acceptance of (for example) sexual promiscuity as normal, and, consequently, right. These assumptions were *built into* the report.

It is unrealistic to say that sociology 'cannot' pronounce on the rightness or wrongness of social behaviour. That would be to assume that sociologists are capable of 'detachment' when studying value-loaded human society. Built into the Christian's sociology, however, will be the assumption that men in society are sinful, and that conflicts, deviance, even certain social institutions, may exist as a result of sin. They are less than ideal; in terms of the creation order, they are abnormal. What 'is' is not necessarily what 'ought' to be.

The essence of sin is disobedience to God. It is our 'natural' condition, and, even as Christians, we find that its effects dog us right to the grave. It is the attempt to be autonomous, to decide for oneself what is right and wrong, and always takes the form of failure to reach God's standards, or of deliberately crossing the boundary of God's law. As we examine society, we dare not overlook the tendency to sin, and we must never forget that our own study will be tainted by that same sin. Sin is pervasive and subtle, it can be both individual and social, and its effects not only displease God, but injure the personality and the group. God's way is not only 'right' in itself, it is the best way.

To take the example of deviance once again: anyone who has picked up a book on the subject will know that the crucial debate is over definitions. What *is* deviant, and what *is* normal? The humanistic sociologist can work only from his own idea of the common humanity, the 'social contract'[2] or some other definition given by society.

Clearly, moral and statistical deviance are different. Problems arise when 'crime', for example, is reduced to 'social deviance', which tends to minimize its moral gravity. The Christian may legitimately (and explicitly) draw his assumptions about normality and deviance from his view of man, and argue his case accordingly. An example from Paul's writing should give a general idea. The Pauline treatment of lying and stealing is couched in terms of a creation ethic, an argument from the God-given structure of society. (And this is why the question of 'origins' is so important.) He told the Christians at Ephesus that each should 'put off falsehood and speak truthfully to his neighbour, for we are all members of one body', and that any who had been stealing must give it up, and instead 'work, doing something useful with his own hands, that he may have something to share with those in need'. It is true that he was writing to the church, but he was using arguments from creation (such as the need to work with one's own hands) and thus applicable to

[2] This idea, which originated with Rousseau, has acquired a certain notoriety since it became part of the British Labour Party's programme. A cynic might say that this serves to illustrate its perennial futility.

all men. Other Old Testament principles, such as the concept of 'neighbour', are there as well, and it is arguable that the New Testament ideas, like the 'members of one body', may also be used as an ideal in the non-Christian world.[3]

Let us take stock, then, of some of the Christian approaches at which we have hinted. Man *is* a kind of slave to society, *not* because he is malleable, *or* because he is a social pawn, but because he is fundamentally a slave to sin, and therefore to a sinful society. This is the reason why Paul encourages the Roman Christians not to let the world (or society, or culture) squeeze them into its mould.[4] This is biblical realism. Man will idolize the myth of freedom (that is, non-Christian freedom) as did Cain when he asked, 'Am I my brother's keeper?' He will only ever achieve, however, a 'formal' freedom. While, as Christians, we ought to make full use of a non-deterministic perspective which takes full account of intentionality, and allows for liberty of choice, we must never confuse this 'liberty' with Christian freedom. The intentionalist perspective makes room for responsibility and accountability: it cannot 'set free'. The distinction between man's idea of freedom (which at root is a pretended autonomy from God's rule) and Christian freedom must be made, in order that the 'glorious liberty' of the latter be realized. And the last point is this. Man is not the arbiter of right and wrong. Although he constantly grasps at autonomy, only God is

[3] *Cf.* Ephesians 4 :: 25, 28 (New International Version).
[4] Romans 12 : 2 (J. B. Phillips).

master, God is king. This is the root of the presuppositional conflicts of the (humanistic) sociological and the Christian world-view.

Whose image?

In brief, then, we have seen that there are different varieties of *homo sociologicus* in social theory. Although writers sometimes give the impression that their particular variety is 'total', none escapes the trap of social relativism, none is a perspective 'from outside'. By contrast, the Christian sociologist uses his biblical view of the total man as a presuppositional base for his sociological theorizing, but never suggests that the social aspect is the whole. However, Christian thought on 'man as image of Maker' *has* tended to neglect the social aspect, which has led to an imbalance in the understanding of man's nature. There is therefore both an internal and an external challenge to Christians studying in the sociological area to get to grips with the meaning of the 'image', and to use in their work the insights gained.

The Christian view of man is inseparable from the Christian's knowledge of God, and although the non-Christian may find much that attracts him in the Christian view, it will not fully make sense to him until he accepts the Christian's God. However, we must continue to assert that man is human only because he is the image of God, and work out the practical implications of this view. Sociological theory should be inseparable from the day-to-day life of man in society: it is meaningless in abstraction. So the Christian view of man must always be shown to be compatible with the real needs of man in society. Asserting the 'image of God' view will not only 'salt' sociological theory, but could, by God's grace, be the means of opening blind eyes to the truth that God is. We must work and pray for the image to be restored, both in ourselves and in others.

Statistics and salvation

At first sight, the sociology of religion has a very threatening appearance to the Christian. There are several reasons for this. One is the comparative novelty of sociological analysis, and its youthful authoritarian stance. Following from this is the fact that sociology seems to 'explain' so many features of Christian belief and practice in its own terms. Another important reason is that sociology shows up so many unimagined snags involved in commitment that one feels less and less inclined to commit oneself to anything. Unintended consequences of Christian teaching have received so much notice that one is constantly aware that there may be features of one's own religion that have gone unnoticed, and yet which stand out a mile to the inquisitive sociologist.

Big problems are raised by the sociological study

of religion, and the fact that these have appeared in other guises before does not really lessen their impact. Over a hundred years ago, for example, when the sociological type of thinking was popular among some German theologians, the Bible was often reduced in status to a social product, comparable to any other literature.

It is somewhat reassuring to notice, though, that the 'problem' feeling has been mutual, and that the phenomenon of religion does perplex sociologists. This might partly explain why the sociology of religion has had such a chequered career. It has never been far from the central concerns of sociology, but for quite a long time (especially after the last war) many sociologists felt that they could say nothing about religion because it was bound up with the unquantifiable entity of belief.

Nowadays, the sociology of religion is flourishing. It has been widely recognized that simply to ignore religion is to reduce one's understanding of man and society. Most people tend to stumble across the sociology of religion either in the form of the endless debate over the link between Protestantism and capitalism, or the arguments about secularization. Still others may be affected via the more colourful or bizarre historical-anthropological accounts of the pursuit of the millennium or the 'Cargo Cults'.[1]

[1] Norman Cohn's fascinating book on medieval millenarianism is called *The Pursuit of the Millennium* (Paladin, 1970). Peter Worsley writes about the Cargo Cults in *The Trumpet Shall Sound* (Paladin, 1970).

A social phenomenon

Sociology views religion as a 'social phenomenon', but as we hope to show, even phrases like this fail to isolate religion for experimental purposes. The 'social phenomenon' approach involves the researcher in looking at manifestations of religious belief, or adherence to a religious group, and speaking about what he sees. Now in a way, the churches themselves use social statistics when they compile a list of communicants, average church attendance at festival times, or quote the national proportion of couples who get married in church. So seeing religion as a social phenomenon is something that we already (perhaps unconsciously) do ourselves.

No sociological definition of religion, however, can fail to contain implications as to the truth of religion. The functionalist, for example, will judge religion according to its effects. That is, religion may seem to have a socially beneficial function in integrating certain groups, or giving meaning to certain institutions, such as marriage. For the Marxian sociologist, on the other hand, religion is automatically judged to be false, because it is based on a false diagnosis of the condition of man. Social problems arise not from the nature of man in relation to God, but from the economic system, the 'mode of production'. Religion thus gives men false hopes of salvation.

The Christian sociologist must take the position of saying that there is 'true' religion manifest in society, and moreover, that there is always *some* form of religion present. He will not ignore the *functions* of religion, or the fact that, for some, religion *is* used as an 'opiate', but neither will he let any of these ideas become his starting-point.

As soon as the sociologist makes his definition of religion, he has, in fact, taken up a position with regard to its character, its truth or falsity, its efficacy or its futility. Naturally enough, not many sociologists attempt to define religion in a few words, so one has to get to grips with different modes of analysis that are used in the study of religion. We shall glance at three approaches here, none of which is mutually exclusive or watertight, but which should give some idea of the ways sociologists look at religion. We shall deliberately use homely and well-known examples for illustration, because we are looking at these ideas on a simple and straightforward level only. But they are examples which should be of interest to every Christian who thinks about his position in society.

Religion as behaviour

This general category is perhaps the most amenable to empirical research. Statistics of religious adherence and practice can readily be obtained, and all manner of conclusions drawn from them. The sociologist may be able to show which ethnic or social group is most likely to be a member of such and such a denomination, or which urban areas are most likely to contain church-attenders. There is evidence, for example, that minority ethnic group (such as West Indians) tend to congregate in the more exuberant Pentecostal groups, and that inhabitants of middle-class suburban areas are far more likely to attend a local church than those of inner-city, working-class areas.

The study of religious behaviour and institutions is often very revealing and sometimes a rebuke to the Christian church. Probably the biggest challenge at the moment is that of class affiliation. Religious activity is often a mark of middle-class status, and the church seems to make very little impact in working-class areas. It is often suggested, moreover, that the church is guilty of proclaiming a 'middle-class gospel', and thus effectively excluding other sectors of the community. The sociologist will want to know why it is that religious beliefs seem to lose plausibility in a certain district of a city, or below a certain income bracket.

The answers to such questions will be given in sociological terms. It may be argued that, due to the nature of their work, manual labourers do not experience the same needs as workers in the professions. Our culture is a very pragmatic one, and the discussion of 'ends' and goals, as opposed to 'means', is educationally limited to a very small number of people. Moreover, many of the words used in talking about values, about death and about God may well be disappearing from the vocabulary of some sectors of society.[2]

The Christian sociologist, while he dares not

[2] See, for example, Alasdair MacIntyre, *Secularization and Moral Change* (OUP, 1967).

ignore the problems thrown up by this kind of sociological study, will approach them with his own presuppositions. He cannot forget when he is doing research in sociology that all men do have a need for salvation in Christ. However, the 'work situation' of different groups may need a lot of exploring: it could be a factor which inhibits the appreciation of fundamental religious needs.

The question of language (in relation to class) is most important, too. Christians deny their message of the free offer of the Good News to all men if they speak in an esoteric language, or have little to do with those who may have different career aspirations from themselves (or rather, who have no career aspirations). The sociologist has a right to expose hypocrisy like this, and Christians must listen. Paul the apostle suggested[3] that the church would be rebuked by the standards of the pagan society around: they would see the blemishes that the church did not. It is sad that the Christian 'answers' to these problems have sometimes been hopeless compromises. On 'language', the answer, for the Christian, can never be simply to abandon any hint of 'redemption', 'sacrifice' or 'atonement'. Rather, the church should explain the gospel (which is, after all, 'the power of God for the salvation of everyone who believes'[4]) without the extra-biblical accretions of sectarian jargon or seventeenth-century usage.

This is not the place to enter these debates, how-

[3] 1 Corinthians 5 : 1.
[4] Romans 1 : 16 (New International Version).

ever; we must simply note that they exist, and begin to work out our own position. It is worth stressing again, though, that although the sociological definition of religion contains implications as to the truth or falsity of religion, it may in other respects be an accurate assessment of the situation. We should never dismiss any sociological 'finding' without thought. What matters is that we be honest and consistent as we use our assumptions to deal with the same problems.

It may appear from the examples given so far that the Christian sociologist must see evangelism as the only task of Christians. Now while evangelism *is* the way that God has chosen to bring people into his family, Christianity is not equivalent to evangelism. The Christian life is to be lived, and it must be seen that the faith affects the whole man. There are other areas touched by the sociologist of religion which deserve much attention. We could mention several of these, but perhaps the most obvious is the very fruitful area of the link between religion and the family. The rites of passage[5] are often still performed in a church context.

The majority of marriages are still solemnized in church buildings, and more than half the babies born in England are still baptized in the Church of England. But what do these rites mean nowadays? Are they still significant to those who participate? There are a lot of questions to which satisfactory answers are still lacking. There is much work for

[5] Weddings, christenings, baptisms or dedications, and funerals.

the committed Christian sociologist, before he even catches up with the others.

Religion as belief

In actual practice the sociologist will go beyond the simple statistical survey with its limited conclusions, and will say something about the social functions of religion. The approach of Durkheim, probably the first 'sociologist of religion', has been most influential.[6]

He drew attention to the functional significance of symbols and ritual in maintaining social integration and cohesion. It is probably this approach, in fact, which has led others to think of communism and psychoanalysis as performing religious *functions* in society. Religious belief is studied as something which gives meaning and plausibility to certain practices and institutions. Death, for example, could be described as the 'gateway to the afterlife', and this description would affect the way in which death was socially accepted. Its social acceptance would be different if it were thought of as annihilation.

The work of Berger and Luckmann (which follows Durkheim and Weber) is important here.[7] They argue that the positivist emphasis in the social sciences has led to a neglect of the subjective realm

[6] E. Durkheim, *The Elementary Forms of Religious Life* (Allen and Unwin, 1971).
[7] P. L. Berger, *The Social Reality of Religion*, and Thomas Luckmann, *The Invisible Religion* (Macmillan N.Y., 1967).

of social reality (as we discussed in relation to 'intentionality'). This neglect was earlier typified by the ignoring of 'religion as belief'. Berger would like to place the sociology of religion in the context of the sociology of knowledge, which, as we noticed before, includes everything that passes for knowledge in society. We could summarize the conclusions from such an outlook as follows.

The sacred formulas and rituals of religion are repeated at crisis times so that the world (or our perception of it) does not get out of control.[8] In order to construct a picture of reality for themselves, people need a system of belief, and religion has a decisive role in maintaining as well as constructing that reality. Once constructed, the strong edifice will provide an insulation from the huge and recurring problems of life. The most acutely felt crises, they would judge, are anomie and death. A 'given' set of rules is most useful, as it helps one sort out priorities and make decisions. A doctrine such as 'immortality' gives hope and comfort to the bereaved, especially when linked to the idea of 'heaven', where they may one day be united with their loved ones. Thus belief can be socially 'explained'.

Sociologists are interested not only in existing beliefs, but also in the declining manifestation of religious belief. The study of secularization is a common theme in most approaches to religious

[8] These writers do not immediately distinguish between magic and religion, which can have a distorting effect on one's view of the latter.

phenomena, and provides one of the major fields of controversy in current theory. The sociologist would ask this kind of question: 'If explicitly religious institutions and symbols have less impact on society and culture today, then what, if anything, is taking their place?'; or, 'What is the true nature of the decline in church attendance? Has it to do with class, education, or some other variable?' There are several fairly recent books on these themes.[9]

Needless to say, Christians should be involved in answering these questions. We must remember that the unbelieving sociologist cannot ultimately break out of his 'social determinism', and can give answers only within the framework of his own language and ideas. His conclusions are not necessarily wrong or untrue, but if the implicit assumption behind his theory is that religion is only something like 'self-transcendence', then we may find that our own presuppositions leave us talking at cross-purposes, not communicating at all. His idea will be that all religion is merely a human construction and, therefore, wishful thinking. The sociological study of religion-as-belief needs much clarification: the Christian is bound to tackle it in a different way from the unbeliever.

We shall just hint at what this means in relation to 'secularization'. If what was said about the intrinsic religiosity of man (chapter four, pp. 63 f.) is

[9] See, for example, B. R. Wilson, *Religion in a Secular Society* (Watts, 1966), or S. Budd, *Sociologists and Religion* (Collier Macmillan, 1973).

true, then this must affect our understanding of the secularization process. For the Christian, secularization means not a 'loss of faith', but a 'relocation of belief'. This is precisely what we suggested in chapter 2, regarding the history of sociology itself. Man's belief was then transferred to, or relocated in, society and man. That is the starting-point, then, of a Christian conception of secularization. Moreover, by showing how this relates to other matters discussed, we can see how distinctive Christian insights in sociology hang together in a relevant way.

Religion as reification

A third approach to religion, which is becoming increasingly popular with the revival of interest in Marxian theory, is that of reification. This refers to the objectifying of a wish for security, maybe for a father-figure, and for the hope of a better world than the present one. Man, especially when he is deprived or oppressed, imagines that there is a 'real' opposite to the situation in which he finds himself, and manufactures a religion. In his alienated condition, he creates (reifies) this false world to compensate for present miseries. The clear implication of this view is that, as religion is an illusion, it is therefore undesirable (misdirecting, as it does, any motivation to build heaven on earth).

Marx himself, who did not believe that religion corresponded to anything 'out there', wrote that it is 'the sigh of the oppressed creature, the heart of a heartless world, the spirit of a spiritless situation'. So the problem, from the point of view of this approach, is neither the changing pattern of religious practice, nor its decline, but rather the very presence of religion. Attention is devoted to the 'social causes' of religion rather than the mere incidence of secularization.

Marx argued that the essence of religion is discovered in philosophy, which exposes the basic alienation of man, showing him to be 'not at home' in the world. The truth of philosophy, in turn, is discovered in politics. Philosophical ideas have always been related to political issues and goals. But political forms themselves are shown to be no more than social relationships, which are characterized by conflict and division. Then, to work the argument back again, we see that to change society so that class divisions and struggles are removed is effectively to render religion obsolete. Marx continues, therefore, 'The abolition of religion, as the illusory happiness of men, is a demand for their real happiness. The call to abandon their illusions about their condition is a call to abandon a condition which requires illusions.'[1]

This, although it is now represented in a more sophisticated clothing, is the basic starting-point for the Marxian sociologist of religion. Admittedly, it is more often 'historical' themes that are given this treatment, but movements such as the so-called

[1] The best single book containing Marx's work is T. B. Bottomore and M. Rubel (ed.), *Karl Marx: Selected Readings in Sociology and Social Philosophy* (Penguin, 1965).

'Jesus People' have given a new impetus to this approach in contemporary studies. For instance, it may be said that the 'Jesus freak' is escaping from the alienation of a less-than-ideal world into a communal paradise which, in fact, exists only in his head. The language of alienation, reification (which is, remember, the alienated man's world-view) and ideology is still very much in vogue.

The mistake that the Marxist tends to make is to imply that his interpretation of religion completely explains its presence and functions. Whilst this mode of analysis yields some useful insights, such as that into the ideological function of religion, it is simply unrealistic to apply it to every situation and expect to find correct answers. The Marxian view does, however, lend itself to debate with the Christian, because the basic assumptions are fairly explicit, and the ground of contention is clear. For example, the Marx–Engels prediction about the continuing rapid decline of religion obstinately refuses to come true. As Christians, we should be doing all we can to relieve their followers of embarrassment by arguing the alternative view. That is, while some men *do* make their own religions they are only counterfeits of true religion, which is God-made: and as God-made, irrepressible.

Christian sociology

6

It must be clear by now that there is a distinctively Christian approach to sociology, and equally clear that at the moment the Christian voice is virtually inaudible in the sociological theatre. I hope that we have shown that it is not sub-Christian to study sociology, and that, on the contrary, we have a duty to 'take every thought captive to obey Christ',[1] and this includes *sociological* thought! Alvin Gouldner, a contemporary sociologist of repute, having rejected the notion that sociological information is neutral, has argued for a self-consciously moral sociology which aims to change society in accordance with its explicit value-system. What a rebuke to Christians! This is exactly what we should be saying – and doing. The challenge is echoing across the valley right now.

[1] 2 Corinthians 10 : 5.

The phrase 'Christian sociology' is certainly not new. There was even a socially conscious bishop who saw the need for a biblically directed Christian sociology back in the 1880s! There have been several attempts to lay the foundations for a Christian sociology since then, and some useful thinking has been done. None, however, has fully got off the ground, and movements have all too often become quickly side-tracked into social action (which is the *partner* of, not the *substitute* for, sociological thinking) or compromised with a sub-biblical 'Christianity'. Only a few individuals have been left to struggle for acceptance, and that with believers and unbelievers alike.

But to talk of Christian sociology today is to court controversy, and to invite scathing criticism. Christians themselves have for a long time been very suspicious of any 'invasion' of the academic world with Christian ideas, for several reasons. They have, for example, swallowed the 'neutral' catchword, and believe that 'detached objectivity' is possible, even in the social sciences. This, if true, would of course rule out Christian sociology. But another reason, equally serious, is that some have imagined that a Christian sociology would claim to be the *only* true way of understanding society, somehow on a par with the infallible Word. While it would be impossible to try to outline a Christian sociology here, we must at least show these objections to be false, suggest how a Christian sociology could emerge, and why, even if it is not called that, it must exist.

We must understand, as I have tried to show, that the consensus of modern sociology is at presuppositional variance with our Christian view of society. Sociology is one product of a world whose values and structures have been relativized. It is a product of the nineteenth-century rejection of a Christian world-view. It has assumed an authority of its own, using 'society' as its only frame of reference. It thus rules out the possibility of, for example, true religion, or the possibility that there is a right way for man to live in society. The sociologist will claim, on the one hand, that he has no right to pronounce on such issues, and on the other, imply by the very style of his writing that he believes sociology has explained the existence of some practice or institution in society. The sociologist *must* make big assumptions about the nature of man and of 'normal social life' in order to offer his sociology as a viable academic discipline. It is at this presuppositional level that debate must take place first of all.

Christian sociology could not possibly be monolithic, or seen as the only way to know the truth about society. Sociology written by non-Christians is still sociology, and very often contains insights with which the Christian must agree. (Unbelievers, after all, *suppress* truth that *is* there, even if in a distorted form.[2]) So non-Christians do not simply peddle 'false' sociology! Never forget that the Christian sociologist, while doing all in his power to avoid error in his work, will inevitably make mis-

[2] Romans 1 : 18.

takes and mar his witness, due to the warping action of remaining sin in his life. Nevertheless, we believe that God has given us his Word and his Spirit, so that we can interpret reality in a true and God-pleasing way.

Perhaps a note on the way we should read the Bible is needed here, although we have touched on this earlier. Christian sociology is not just 'ordinary' sociology sprinkled with apposite proof texts! The Bible is God's Word to man, and is to be regarded as consistent, coherent and absolutely authoritative. We must rely on the Holy Spirit to enable us to understand the Bible, and therefore approach it humbly, prepared to be found wanting ourselves. It is important to appreciate the context of particular teachings, and yet to see that the teaching is 'from outside'. It did not *originate* with human writers. Above all, the Bible must be seen as a whole, integrated book, and the details viewed in the perspective of the central themes of creation, redemption, the Lordship of Christ, and so on. Only in this way will we be able to sort out our own presuppositions about man and society, and then use them as a base for our sociology.

To sum this up: by 'Christian sociology' we do not mean a sociology that is utterly oblivious to all 'non-Christian' sociology, but rather one which develops its distinctive sociological presuppositions, and uses these to criticize or modify other sociologies. There is also scope for distinctively Christian, alternative sociological theory. The abuse of the idea would be to turn sociology into

87

a new sectarian weapon – and that is certainly not the intention behind the use of the term. To talk merely of Christians *in* sociology, however, would be to imply the Christian/sociologist role-split which, as we have seen, is unsound from both a Christian and a sociological point of view. It denies, on the one hand, that Christ is Lord of our sociological imagination; and denies, on the other, that our Christian presuppositions have any relevance to our lives as sociologists. Thus we would defend the qualified use of the term 'Christian sociology'.

If only Christians were proud of the Good News, unashamed of their biblical world-view, and willing to contend for Christian presuppositions in the sociological arena! As in every other activity, we should pray that the Spirit of God might fill us as Christian students of sociology. We urgently need the 'Christian mind'[3] as we view society in all its complexity and its increasing distance from divinely given norms and values. The sovereignty of God is not a 'theoretical' doctrine, but rather a practical incentive for Christians to stake out new areas for their Lord.

With tact and gentle authority we have an obligation to lay bare the inadequacy of any theory which admits nothing beyond the positivistic or the naturalistic. In the last analysis the evidence for the truth of our world-view is not to be found in superior theories (which, carelessly handled, could

[3] *The Christian Mind* (SPCK, 1963) is the title of an excellent book by Harry Blamires, in which he pleads for Christians to think 'Christianly' *all* the time.

simply look like condescending dogmatism) but in changed lives. The Christian sociologist should be marked by his humility, his honesty and his intellectual integrity, both in his life and his writing.

The apostle Peter sums it up: 'Always be prepared to make a defence to any one who calls you to account for the hope that is in you, yet do it with gentleness and reverence; and keep your conscience clear, so that, when you are abused, those who revile your good behaviour in Christ may be put to shame.'[4]

[4] I Peter 3 : 15–16.

Glossary

Anomie is a state of 'normlessness'; of having no accepted behaviour pattern to which to conform.

Behaviourism is the study of human (or other) conduct in response to stimuli, usually under controlled conditions.

Determinism is the doctrine that all things are determined by causes; economic determinism suggests that economic forces give rise to the same outcome everywhere.

Deviance is the departure from social norms and values.

Empiricism is the doctrine that knowledge is obtained from experience only, *i.e.* by experimentation.

Internalization is the learning of things so that they become habits, skills, beliefs and opinions.

Naturalism is the doctrine which systematically rejects the supernatural.

Secularization is the process whereby religious beliefs, practices and institutions lose social significance. See pp. 80 ff.

Socialization is the transmission of culture, the process whereby men learn the rules and practices of social groups. See p. 51.

Further reading

Abraham Kuyper, *Lectures on Calvinism* (Eerdmans, 1931). A book which every Christian student would do well to read. Kuyper shows clearly the relationship between the Bible, Christian faith and one's world-view. Do not be put off by either the fact that the lectures were given in the 1890s, or the title!

David O. Moberg, *The Great Reversal* (SU, 1973); R. Behm and C. Salley, *Your God Is Too White* (InterVarsity Press, 1970; Lion Publishing, 1973). These are two American books which use a sociological perspective to expose contradictions in Christianity. The former is on the false dichotomy between evangelism and social concern, and the latter on the church's compromise with institutionalized racism.

G.C. Berkouwer, *Man: The Image of God* (Eerdmans, 1952; Inter-Varsity Press, England, 1973). An excellent and reliable treatment of the biblical view of man, by an outstanding Dutch philosopher-theologian. It is full of insight relevant to the sociologist.

David Martin, *Fifty Key Words in Sociology* (Lutterworth, 1972). A useful little dictionary which explains simply the sociological usage of words. A boon to anyone frustrated by obscure jargon.